# The Lost Colony of Roanoke

Unraveling the Mystery of the Vanished Settlement

**CCM Waterston-Hillier**

**Listed & Published on www.interestingbooks.store**

# Check out other exciting titles

# Table of Contents


FOREWORD ........................................................................... 1

**CHAPTER 1: THE ROANOKE EXPEDITION (1587)** ................. 4

A World In Transition ........................................................ 5

The Age Of Exploration .................................................... 5

The English Empire's Aspirations ...................................... 7

Sir Walter Raleigh: The Visionary Leader ......................... 7

Raleigh's Grand Plan ........................................................ 8

Challenges Of The New World .......................................... 9

The Courage And Determination Of The Settlers .............. 11

**CHAPTER 2: THE ARRIVAL ON ROANOKE** ...................... 12

A New Beginning .............................................................. 13

The Challenges of Settlement ........................................... 14

Shelter and Survival ........................................................ 15

Interactions with Native Tribes ........................................ 15

John White's Leadership ................................................... 16

Efforts to Secure Supplies and Support ............................ 16

**CHAPTER 3: THE DISAPPEARANCE** ............................... 19

Circumstances Leading to Delayed Supplies ..................... 19

Growing Concerns and Dwindling Resources .................... 20

The Return of John White in the Year 1590 ....................... 22

The Shocking Discovery ................................................... 22

**CHAPTER 4: THEORIES AND SPECULATIONS** ................. 25

Relocation ....................................................................... 25

Assimilation ..................................................................... 27

Conflict with Native Americans ........................................ 28

Enduring Mysteries and Unanswered Questions ............... 29

Modern Research and Discoveries ...............................................31

**Chapter 5: Archaeological Discoveries** .........................................**32**

Excavations at the Roanoke Site...............................................34

Significant Findings ....................................................................34

Insights into Daily Life and John White's Role ........................38

**Chapter 6: Native American Perspectives and Modern Investigations...43**

The Croatoan Tribe and Their Possible Role.............................44

Native American Oral Histories ................................................46

Modern Technology: LiDAR and DNA Analysis.......................47

Recent Expeditions and Contemporary Findings......................49

**Conclusion**..................................................................................**52**

Unraveling the Enigma and the Legacy of Roanoke................52

The Complexity and Uncertainty of the Roanoke Colony Mystery........52

The Enduring Fascination and Cultural Impact of Roanoke ..................54

The Call for Continued Research and Exploration....................56

# FOREWORD

**Dear Reader,**

Welcome to *"The Lost Colony of Roanoke: Unraveling the Mystery of the Vanished Settlement"!* This book takes you on a journey through one of the most intriguing mysteries in American history. The story of the Roanoke Colony has fascinated people for centuries, and this book delves deep into the mystery to uncover the truth behind the vanished settlement.

The Roanoke Colony was established in 1587 by Sir Walter Raleigh, an English explorer and soldier who was granted a charter by Queen Elizabeth I to establish a colony in the New World. The colony was located on Roanoke Island, off the coast of what is now North Carolina. The settlers were led by John White, an artist and cartographer who had previously been to the New World with Raleigh's earlier expeditions.

The initial settlement was small, with only around 100 people, but it was intended to be the first step in establishing a permanent English presence in the New World. However, things did not go as planned. The settlers faced challenges, including hostile Native American tribes, harsh weather conditions, and a lack of supplies. In 1588, John White returned to England to request assistance from Raleigh and the English government, leaving behind his wife and daughter, who had given birth to a granddaughter, Virginia Dare, the first English child born in the New World.

When White returned to Roanoke in 1590, he found the colony abandoned. There was no sign of the settlers; the only clue was the word "Croatoan" carved into a tree. The fate of the Roanoke Colony has remained a mystery ever since, with numerous theories and hypotheses put forward over the years.

Through meticulous research and analysis, the authors of this book have pieced together the events leading up to the disappearance of the Roanoke Colony. They explore the various theories and hypotheses put forward over the years, from the idea that Native Americans killed the settlers to the possibility that they were absorbed into local tribes or even made their way to other parts of the New World.

The book also provides a fascinating insight into the

world of the late 16th century, a time of exploration and territorial expansion. It explores the motivations behind Raleigh's quest for dominance in the New World and the other major European countries engaged in the fight for supremacy. It also looks at the exotic treasures the New World promised, from gold and silver to new plants and animals.

Whether you are a history buff, mystery enthusiast, or someone who loves a good story, "The Lost Colony of Roanoke" will captivate and intrigue you. The authors have done an excellent job of bringing the story of the Roanoke Colony to life, painting a vivid picture of the challenges faced by the settlers and the world they lived in.

One of this book's strengths is balancing historical accuracy with readability. The authors have done their research, but they present the information in a way that is accessible and engaging. They also do an excellent job of separating fact from fiction, debunking some of the more outlandish theories that have been put forward over the years.

Overall, *The Lost Colony of Roanoke* is a must-read for anyone interested in American history, mystery, or exploration. It provides a fascinating insight into one of the most enduring mysteries in American history, and it does so in an informative and entertaining way. So, if you're looking for a book that will keep you on the edge of your seat, look no further than *"The Lost Colony of Roanoke: Unraveling the Mystery of the Vanished Settlement."*


**Sincerely,**

**CCM Waterston-Hillier**

# CHAPTER 1

## The Roanoke Expedition (1587)

## A World in Transition

Late in the 16th century, it was a time of dramatic change in Europe and other parts of the world. This era was characterized by brave and ambitious exploration when the amount of the known globe increased astoundingly. It was an age of bold explorers and far-reaching aspirations, and it was against this background that the English Empire, headed by the visionary Sir Walter Raleigh, cast its eyes beyond the Atlantic Ocean to the unexplored areas of the New World. Sir Walter Raleigh, a visionary, led the English Empire.

## The Age of Exploration

At the end of the 16th century, there was a widespread

yearning worldwide for exploration and territorial expansion. The major European countries were engaged in a cutthroat fight for dominance and sought ways to expand their influence farther afield. The New World was a vast and mysterious expanse that promised great riches, unknown lands, and exotic treasures waiting to be seized.

The maps of the known globe had already started to be redrawn by the time Christopher Columbus set sail for the Americas, which is evidence that there was more to explore beyond the horizon. The voyage of the globe by Ferdinand Magellan had broken the confines of the known world, proving that new frontiers awaited those who were brave enough to seek them out. Sir Francis Drake, a fearless English explorer who became a legendary figure during his time for sailing across the world and stealing wealth from Spain, is credited with establishing England as a world power.

Many people's hearts were set on becoming rich, famous, and having exciting adventures at a period when Europe was turning its gaze toward the rest of the world. It was the beginning of the Age of Discovery, which would irrevocably alter the path that history would take from that point on.

# The English Empire's Aspirations

Under the patronage of Queen Elizabeth I, England was keen to guarantee its position in this developing drama amidst the zeal for exploration and development that was taking place at the time. The English crown was interested in discovering new trade routes, unknown lands, and the legendary Northwest Passage, a way to Asia's wealth. With all its untapped possibilities, the New World beckoned, and Sir Walter Raleigh was selected to head the expedition.

# Sir Walter Raleigh: The Visionary Leader

Sir Walter Raleigh, a man of extraordinary insight and drive, was the driving force behind this bold enterprise. Raleigh was born in 1552, and his life is a tribute to the endless possibilities that the Age of Discovery gave to those who had the bravery to dream. Raleigh's life was a testament to the unlimited possibilities of the Age of Discovery.

While serving as a soldier in Ireland, Raleigh's interest in the New World was sparked, which led to his eventual exploration of that region. He was the first to hear stories of undiscovered territories to the west, places abounding with riches and opportunity. These lands were said to be unexplored. These tales stoked the fire inside him, and he was soon completely enamored with the concept of founding an English colony in the Americas.

Raleigh got a charter with the unshakable backing of Queen Elizabeth I. This charter gave Raleigh the power to explore, colonize, and administer any "remote, heathen and barbarous lands, countries, and territories, not possessed of any Christian prince, nor inhabited by Christian people." Raleigh secured this charter because of Queen Elizabeth I's support. This charter was a permission to dream on a scale that had never been seen before, and it gave the English a chance to influence the future of their fledgling empire.

## Raleigh's Grand Plan

The ambitious goal that Raleigh set for himself was to create an everlasting English presence in the New World, which was nothing short of awe-inspiring. In 1584, he embarked on two expeditions to the coast of North America to investigate the areas that would eventually be referred to as Virginia and North Carolina. These excursions exposed the region's astounding natural beauty and validated the possibility of settling there.

Roanoke Island was the location of Sir Walter Raleigh's first effort at colonization, which took place the following year in 1585. However, this first endeavor was met with many difficulties, including disputes with native peoples, a lack of resources, and poor living circumstances. Ultimately, the colonists were compelled to give up their nascent town and return to England. On their way back, they left behind the ruins of their unsuccessful enterprise.

But this defeat did not discourage Raleigh in the least. His resolve would not waver, and in the year 1587, he planned a second trip to Roanoke Island, this time with John White serving as the captain. Their goal was to establish a colony that would last longer. This time, in addition to males, the initiative would involve women and children, indicating a more genuine commitment to permanent colonization.

## Challenges of the New World

The early English immigrants in the New World faced enormous difficulties when they arrived in the New World. They were setting off on a voyage into a region far different from where they came from, a land full of unknowns and potential dangers for them. They were faced with several significant obstacles, including the following:

## 1. Harsh Conditions

Roanoke Island was a wild location that had not been tamed by humans and was characterized by hazardous marshes, thick woods, and flora and wildlife that were foreign to them. The early settlers had to fight not only with the unpredictability of the forces of nature, such as storms but also with the constant battle for existence in a harsh and brutal environment.

## 2. Limited Resources

The supplies that came from England were unreliable and often not enough. The colonists were forced to depend on the limited resources of their new environment, which presented them with the ongoing issue of acquiring sufficient amounts of food and fresh water to ensure their survival.

## 3. Unfamiliar Territory

The settlers from Roanoke were venturing into territory about which they had little to no prior information. They were forced to adjust to a completely alien landscape and converse with native peoples whose languages, rituals, and practices were utterly strange to them. The gap in cultural and language understanding provided significant challenges to the possibility of harmonious cohabitation.

## The Courage and Determination of the Settlers

The settlers who started on this risky voyage displayed amazing bravery and unflinching perseverance despite the severe hurdles they faced. They were compelled to set sail for the New World by a great feeling of adventure, a passionate conviction in Raleigh's mission, and a yearning for a better life in the region. People from many walks of life and armed with a wide range of expertise were included in their number, but they were bound together by the goal of establishing a new life in a foreign country.

Their trip was more than just a test of their physical abilities; it also demonstrated the power of the human spirit. It was a journey into the unknown, propelled by aspiration, optimism, and an unquenchable hunger for the remarkable. The indomitable spirit of exploration and discovery that defined the late 16th century may be seen in the colonists' dogged resolve to establish a footing in the New World despite their enormous challenges. This is a monument to the spirit of exploration and discovery that characterized the late 16th century.

In 1587, when the ships bringing the colonists reached the beaches of Roanoke Island, they carried the people on board and the hopes and ambitions of a whole country. They had no idea their tale would develop into a captivating, lasting mystery that would mesmerize generations and motivate the dogged quest for answers. The Roanoke Expedition of 1587 was more than simply a chapter in history; it was the prologue to a legend that continues to call us into the heart of the unknown, where the bravery of the past meets the curiosity of the present. In other words, the Roanoke Expedition of 1587 was the beginning of a tale.

# CHAPTER 2

## The Arrival on Roanoke

Roanoke Island, a green gem situated among the immense expanse of the Atlantic Ocean, became visible on the horizon in 1587. Here, against the background of this untamed wilderness, 118 colonists, including women and children, stepped on the beaches of what would become a crucible of their ambitions and hardships. This place was significant because it was the first place the English settled in North America. Their arrival signaled the start of a new chapter that would put their resiliency, drive, and capacity to manage the complexity of this new world to the test.

## A New Beginning

English colonists' settlement of this land marked the beginning of a new period in the English colonial presence in the Americas. This voyage, led by John White, differed from the ones before it because it was possible for long-term settlement. Families had joined the ranks, which was a statement that they were dedicated to discovering and forming a flourishing English community on these faraway seas.

The colonists must have experienced a range of feelings when they landed from their ships onto the sandy beaches of Roanoke Island. These feelings would have included exhilaration at the possibility of beginning a new life, dread in the face of a relentless environment, and optimism that their sacrifices would result in a wealthy future.

## The Challenges of Settlement

The difficulties in store for the colonists of Roanoke were on par with those presented by the surrounding forest. The familiar English landscapes they had just fled stood in sharp contrast to the unfamiliar environment of Roanoke Island, which was covered in thick woods and swampy terrain. They made the construction of a haven and a basic support system for themselves their priority to ensure their continued existence.

# Shelter and Survival

The settlers had few resources and no quick restocking methods, so they were confronted with building shelters and deriving their food from the soil. The construction of homes and defenses became a top priority, and every available hand was required for this labor-intensive task. The fight for existence extended to acquiring food and fresh water, which often included foraging and hunting in a foreign environment. Every day was an uphill struggle against the harsh truths of nature.

# Interactions with Native Tribes

On this wild island, the colonists from Roanoke were not the only people living there. Many indigenous Algonquian-speaking tribes lived in the surrounding territories, including the Croatoan and the Secotan. These contacts were like a double-edged sword because although some indigenous communities welcomed the English, offered help, and facilitated commerce with them, others viewed the English with distrust, leading to confrontations between the two groups.

As the governor of the colony, John White was compelled to take on the responsibilities of both a mediator and a diplomat. His abilities as a diplomat were tested as he attempted to forge alliances and win the favor of the indigenous people. A successful outcome in these exchanges was essential because it may determine whether or not there would be peace and tranquility in this unfamiliar place.

## John White's Leadership

John White, a man with a wide range of skills, played an important role in the Roanoke colony's attempts to create a base of operations in the New World. In addition to administrative responsibilities, as governor, he had a significant part in determining the course of events for the colony.

## Efforts to Secure Supplies and Support

White was tasked with obtaining supplies and help from England, one of his most important jobs. The colony's continued existence depended on a consistent food supply; however, this proved extremely difficult due to the unpredictability of transatlantic travel. White, realizing the critical nature of the situation, made the unfortunate choice in

1587 to go back to England in search of the aid that was so sorely required. He took his wife and children, leaving the colonists behind.

His departure was a courageous demonstration of leadership and a very moving instance of self-sacrifice. He had no idea that upon his return to England, he would be met with unanticipated challenges, one of which would be the commencement of war between England and Spain. These occurrences would put a major delay on his trip back to Roanoke, changing history's direction.

When John White's ship sailed out into the distance beyond the horizon, he left behind a precariously balanced colony on the edge of hope and trepidation. Establishing a community in an untamed country presented enormous hurdles, and the future of the Roanoke colony hung in the balance as it waited for the pages of history to tell its final destiny.

On the beaches of Roanoke Island, the tale of these colonists, their dealings with the indigenous peoples, and John White's position as governor and diplomat would continue to develop. It was a voyage that would put their mettle to the test, allow them to establish new connections, and mark the beginning of a legacy that would reverberate through the annals of time. This legacy would one day become the mystery surrounding the Lost Colony of Roanoke.

# CHAPTER 3

## The Disappearance

In the annals of the history of the Roanoke colony, the year 1590 is remembered as a tragic turning point. Three years had passed since John White had unwillingly said goodbye to the settlers who had settled on Roanoke Island, leaving them with the promise that he would return soon with much-needed supplies. However, due to a confluence of unanticipated events and an unstable time in England, a shroud of mystery and ambiguity was cast over the outcome of the colony's situation.

## Circumstances Leading to Delayed Supplies

The turbulent events that were taking on in England were mainly to blame for the delay in the return of the supply ships, which was a lifeline that the Roanoke colony anxiously anticipated. When John White embarked on his voyage to return to England in the year 1587, he had no way of knowing the difficulties that awaited him once he reached his destination.

During this time, England was actively involved in several foreign wars, the most notable of which was their war with Spain. This conflict required the entire attention of the English crown and its resources, diverting attention away from the predicament the Roanoke colonists found themselves in. The continuing battles burdened England's naval resources, making it harder to assign ships and supplies to the far-flung colony.

The plight of the Roanoke colonists faded into oblivion in the upheaval caused by the unfolding of world events. The lengthy delay in the return of the widely awaited supplies was caused by a lack of available ships, resources, and men, in addition to the urgent demands of a country that was now engaged in a conflict.

## Growing Concerns and Dwindling Resources

Back on Roanoke Island, the colonists were met with a growing feeling of dread and hopelessness as the passing of the months evolved into the passing of the years without any indication of the relief they needed. Their already restricted resources were further decreased to alarmingly low levels due to their actions. The fight for survival turned into a daily hardship, and the relentless circumstances of the New World offered little compassion to those who suffered under them.

Because their supplies had run out, the colonists had no alternative but to depend on what little resources the island could provide them. These resources were very limited. It wasn't long until fishing, hunting, and foraging were more than simply a way of life; they were essential to staying alive. The colonists were adept at adjusting to the opportunities presented by the terrain, but the prospect of limited resources and unpredictability hung big over their heads.

During this challenging time, their contacts with the local Algonquian-speaking tribes, especially the Croatoan and Secotan members, were more important. The colonists forged relationships with the local indigenous populations to survive the difficult conditions of Roanoke Island's wilderness. These villages served as a lifeline for the colonists.

# The Return of John White in the Year 1590

John White, carrying the weight of the colony's responsibilities and aspirations, ultimately managed to gain passage back to Roanoke Island in 1590. His travels had been challenging, ambiguous, and littered with impediments to his progress. However, he made it through the most difficult times because of his unyielding drive to get back together with the colonists and provide them with long-awaited supplies.

On the other hand, when John White arrived on Roanoke Island, he was confronted with a horrifying reality that took his breath away. The colony, which was once alive with the bustling activities of English settlers, had fallen into an eerie silence since it had been abandoned. It seemed as if all signs of life had been snuffed out in this once hopeful community.

# The Shocking Discovery

The more John White proceeded into the town, the more his heart sunk with each deserted home and route obscured by overgrowth. There was no sign of the colonists, not even the sounds of youngsters playing or adults doing their everyday activities. It was as if they had dissipated into thin air, leaving only traces of their existence in echoes.

In the middle of an increasing dread, John White came upon a puzzling and perplexing hint in the form of a single word carved into a tree: "CROATOAN." This obtuse statement sent chills down his spine and added another mystery to the predicament the colonists found themselves in. The term "Croatoan" gave the impression that the colonists had moved, most likely to Croatoan Island, a neighboring region that the Croatoan people inhabited. Nevertheless, there was no clarity, and the message raised more questions than answers.

When he was forced to make an excruciating choice, John White was in shock and uncertain. Should he seek the colonists on Croatoan Island, putting his life and crew's lives in danger, or should he return to England with the haunting mystery of the Lost Colony of Roanoke? As he struggled with the unanswered issue of what had happened to the missing settlers and the lingering mystery of what had occurred during those fateful years on Roanoke Island, the mystery of the disappeared settlers would continue to torment him.

The disappearance of the Roanoke colonists is still one of the most puzzling events in human history. This enigma has persisted for centuries, pushing successive generations to try to solve the mystery and discover the hidden truths buried deep below Roanoke Island's thick vegetation.

# CHAPTER 4

## Theories and Speculations

The captivating enigma of what happened to the Roanoke colony in 1590 and why it has not been solved despite decades of investigation and speculation by historians, archaeologists, and history buffs. The mysterious dissolution of the colony has given rise to several hypotheses and conjectures, each of which provides a unique point of view on the historical problem it seeks to solve.

## Relocation

Theory: There is a widely held belief that the Roanoke colonists, who were confronted with diminishing resources and unclear prospects on the island, may have decided to go to a new place in the hopes of finding more favorable conditions for their continued existence.

## The Lost Colony of Roanoke

Supporting Evidence: The word "CROATOAN" was carved into a tree, and some historical sources claim that this might have been a hint left by the colonists to indicate their plan to migrate to Croatoan Island, where they had developed cordial connections with the Croatoan people. In addition, successive expeditions in the region recorded sightings of people with European traits among the Native American tribes, which added fuel to the fire of conjecture that the colonists had assimilated with the indigenous cultures.

The idea that the colonists moved to other areas is intriguing because it provides a glimmer of hope that they may have found safety elsewhere. It is consistent with the notion that they were resourceful and adaptive, ready to make bold efforts to secure their survival in an environment that was foreign to them and presented several challenges.

However, the relocation notion also raises concerns over whether such a shift is possible. Did the colonists have the resources necessary to go on such a lengthy journey? What difficulties may they have had if they had moved to a different place? If they have moved, why haven't they left clearer hints about where they have gone?

# Assimilation

**Theory**: There is also the possibility that the Roanoke colonists eventually became integrated with the native tribes, taking on their culture, traditions, and way of life as their own over time.

**Supporting Evidence:** There are historical stories of persons who seem European being met among Native American tribes in the area. These historical accounts are from the past. According to these tales, it is possible that some of the colonists intermarried and assimilated themselves into the native populations. Archaeological data, such as objects from Europe discovered among Native American holdings, supports the theory that cultural interchange may have occurred.

The assimilation idea highlights the flexibility of the Roanoke colonists and the possibilities for harmonious living with the area's residents. It gives the impression of resiliency and endurance achieved via cultural assimilation.

Nonetheless, this hypothesis is fraught with difficulties regarding the historical data it necessitates. Suppose the colonists were successful in being assimilated into the local tribes. In that case, this may have resulted in fewer traces in the historical record, making it more difficult to establish what happened to them. In addition, doubts emerge over how the colonists would have voluntarily adopted such a significant change in cultural norms.

## Conflict with Native Americans

**Theory:** According to this hypothesis, the colonists from Roanoke may have been driven out of their settlement due to hostility or battles fought with native tribes.

**Supporting Evidence:** The historical records suggest disagreements between the English settlers and some local tribes, especially the Secotan. Evidence suggests that relations deteriorated, and fights took place as a result. Even while there is no hard evidence to suggest that there would be a large-scale battle, it is impossible to rule out the prospect of smaller-scale conflicts.

The conflict hypothesis depicts the colonists of Roanoke in a more bleak and sad light than the alternative explanation. It conjures the prospect of bloodshed and misery, implying that the English settlers may have faced opposition from the native tribes, which may have eventually led to the death or dispersal of the native tribes.

This hypothesis is not devoid of any difficulties. The historical record does not give conclusive proof of a big, violent war during the period in question. In addition, it is still not quite apparent why the colonists did not leave more obvious signals of anguish or peril if an adversarial force had confronted them.

# Enduring Mysteries and Unanswered Questions

The departure of the Roanoke colony is still cloaked in lingering mystery, and many issues remain unsolved. The following are important aspects of the mystery:

## The Fate of the Colonists

What happened to the colonists who settled in Roanoke is unknown. Were they able to successfully relocate or assimilate into their new environment, or did they have to contend with unfortunate events? Researchers and historians can still not clearly understand what happened since insufficient proof exists.

# CROATOAN

The cryptic message "CROATOAN" raises questions about the colonists' intentions. Was it a warning of danger, or did it indicate that they had arrived at their destination? The very nature of the term invites interpretation and conjecture since it functions as both a hint and a mystery simultaneously.

## Evidence of the Past

It isn't easy to come to any firm conclusions regarding what happened to the Roanoke colony during the 16th century since there is so little physical evidence from that period. Although there have been discoveries of items related to the colony, a complete understanding of what happened to it has not been established.

## Historical Records

The reconstruction of the circumstances that led up to the colony's abandonment is made more difficult by the existence of historical sources that are either incomplete or, on occasion, conflicting. The fact that the colonists write no in-depth narratives contributes to the air of mystery.

# Modern Research and Discoveries

Utilizing cutting-edge technology and multidisciplinary methodologies, recent studies and findings have given fresh light on the enigma of Roanoke:

## <u>Archaeological Excavations</u>

At the Roanoke site, ongoing archaeological investigations have found new items and evidence, offering insights into everyday life in the colony and perhaps revealing connections with Native Americans. These digs continue to turn up useful material and provide new insights into the past that were previously unavailable.

## <u>LiDAR and DNA Analysis</u>

The use of cutting-edge technology, like LiDAR scanning and DNA analysis, has been put to use in the investigation of any buried clues and genetic links between the descendants of colonists and members of native tribes. These cutting-edge methodologies can unearth facts concealed for a long time and solve the enigma.

## <u>Contemporary Expeditions</u>

Recent excursions to Roanoke Island and the surrounding areas have brought current discoveries and a recommitment to unraveling the enigma. Researchers and hobbyists continue to investigate the area to discover answers to questions that have confounded previous generations.

Even though the disappearance of the Roanoke colony is often considered one of the most puzzling events in human history, the combination of historical documents, archaeological findings, and contemporary research methodologies continues to propel the hunt for answers. The everlasting interest in the Lost Colony of Roanoke continues, and many hope that discoveries may one day solve the mysteries surrounding this mystery that date back hundreds of years.

The Roanoke mystery is a monument to the continuing fascination of unsolved enigmas and the human need to find the truth, however elusive it may be, even as we dive further into the annals of history and embrace the possibilities given by contemporary science.

# CHAPTER 5

## Archaeological Discoveries

The mystery surrounding the disappearance of the Roanoke colony has long captivated the imaginations of historians, archaeologists, and fans alike. The colony was located in what is now the state of North Carolina. Extensive archaeological digs have been carried out at the Roanoke site to uncover the enigma surrounding this vanished community. These digs have uncovered many artifacts, buildings, and clues that give priceless insights into the life of the English settlers who once called Roanoke Island home. These people first arrived on the island in the 16th century. This chapter takes a deep dive into the field of archaeological discovery, emphasizing key discoveries such as pieces of pottery, tools, and the location of the first fort. In addition, we will investigate how these findings provide nuanced views into everyday life inside the colony and the essential role that John White played, both as a colonist and as a well-known cartographer.

## Excavations at the Roanoke Site

Since the beginning of the archaeological investigation, the Roanoke site, which may be found on Roanoke Island in North Carolina, has been one of the most important locations. These excavations have been conducted to discover the physical relics of the colony's existence. Over time, they have discovered a treasure trove of historical items and buildings.

Archaeologists have been conducting careful and deliberate excavations, burrowing down into the earth to discover hints that may provide information about what happened to the vanished colony. These excavations have often included a significant amount of manual effort, with archaeologists meticulously sorting through many layers of soil to discover relics of the past that had been buried for several years.

## Significant Findings

### 1. Pottery Shards

The pottery fragments found at the Roanoke site are

among the most important discoveries. These pieces of broken pottery containers provide a priceless glimpse into the routine activities and traditions of the Roanoke colonists and their culture. Archaeologists can get insight into the colonists' European origins and their struggles to adjust to life in the New World by evaluating the pottery's style, design, and production skills. This allows the archaeologists to understand the colonists better.

Broken pieces of pottery provide a wealth of information when pieced together. They lighten the colonists' many containers for eating, cooking, and storing. The aesthetic preferences of the colonists and the cultural influences that formed their ceramics may be deduced from the patterns and motifs on these pottery shards. These clay pieces provide a tale of everyday life by elucidating what the colonists ate, how they prepared their food, and the containers they used for their meals.

In addition, the discovery of broken pieces of pottery with a European aesthetic demonstrates the tenacity of the early colonists. Despite the severe circumstances and the relative seclusion of their new habitat, they produced ceramics in styles they knew from Europe, contributing to preserving aspects of their European identity. This tenacity in cultural traditions in the face of the obstacles posed by colonization is evidence of the adaptability and resolve of the colonists.

## 2. Tools and Implements

The excavations at the Roanoke site have also resulted in the discovering of various artifacts and tools. These discoveries include many items made of metal, such as nails, and a variety of instruments used in building and day-to-day activities. These artifacts provide concrete proof that the colonists were resourceful and able to adjust to the difficulties presented by their new environment.

The artifacts, such as tools and implements, that archaeologists discovered provide insights into the practical elements of day-to-day living inside the colony. These artifacts demonstrate the colonists' dependence on technology and artistry to construct buildings, produce commodities, and maintain their way of life. Because of the scarcity of resources on Roanoke Island, the colonists had to be resourceful and inventive to make the most of what they had. The discovery of metal artifacts provides evidence of this degree of industry and creativity.

These hammers, saws, and other instruments each have a tale to tell about tenacity and finding solutions to challenges. They represent the colonists' perseverance to carve out a living for themselves in a strange area and their dedication to constructing a community despite their challenges.

## 3. The First Fort Site

The location of the first fort that the Roanoke colonists built is one of the most important discoveries that has come out of the Roanoke archaeological field in recent years. This fort, often called "Site X," is very important historically. It also provides important insights into the structure and organization of the early town and looks into where the colonists originally established their presence on the island.

A tangible trace of the origins of the Roanoke colony may be found at the location that archaeologists have named Site X. It is a crucial part of the jigsaw because it shows exactly where the colonists arrived on Roanoke Island for the first time and where they started building their town. The fort's configuration, dimensions, and characteristics provide crucial insights into the early phases of the colony's life.

The researchers have been able to rebuild the fort's plan and get some understanding of its function as a result of their meticulous excavation and study efforts. The colonists wanted to secure themselves and establish a foothold in the New World. The ruins of defensive constructions and the placement of numerous artifacts inside the fort reveal information about how the colonists attempted to do this.

## Insights into Daily Life and John White's Role

The Roanoke colony's everyday life may be pieced together using the information these archaeological finds provide to create a vibrant and detailed mosaic. They take us back in time and enable us to picture the problems the colonists faced and the victories they achieved as they adapted to the difficulties of their new surroundings.

### The Pottery's Culinary Clues

An intriguing look into the colonists' gastronomic practices may be garnered from the ceramic fragments collected from the site. Evidence of cooking procedures, food storage habits, and eating practices may be deduced from the kinds of containers used and the wear patterns on the ceramics. Researchers can determine whether the colonists cooked their food in open hearths or enclosed ovens, the sorts of food they made, and even the spices and ingredients they used in their meals by looking at the food and how they cooked it.

Archaeologists can replicate the sensory experiences of the Roanoke colony by analyzing the ceramics from the settlement. This includes the smells that wafted from their cooking pots and the flavors of the foods they relished. These hints about cuisine contribute to a deeper comprehension of the nutrition of the colonists as well as their attempts to modify European recipes to accommodate the ingredients and techniques readily accessible in the New World.

## Tools: Testaments to Industry

The colonists' perseverance and ability to make do with what they had is abundantly clear from the tools and implements found at the Roanoke site. They symbolize the colonists' capacity to make and mend the necessary objects for everyday living, such as constructing homes and making household products. Metal tools hint at a certain degree of crafting expertise, enabling the colonists to complete various projects.

These implements and tools are more than simply antiques; they are testimonies to the resolve of the early settlers to construct a new existence in an environment that presented several challenges. Every tool has a history, from the nails used to construct buildings to the woodworking tools used to fashion the furniture and implements utilized in the colony. Collectively, they look into the handwork and skill that kept the Roanoke town afloat throughout its history.

## The First Fort: A Foundation of Hope

The location of the initial fort, referred to as "Site X," was a historic discovery that will echo throughout the annals of Roanoke history. It puts us in the colonists' position as they began their risky trip into the unknown and enables us to put ourselves in their shoes. Both the location and construction of the fort indicate the settlers' fears for their safety and their ambition to build a stronghold in this new and uncharted territory.

As a representation of perseverance and optimism, Site X is an important landmark. It is evidence that the colonists had faith in the opportunities presented by the New World and were unyielding in their dedication to constructing a society capable of withstanding the difficulties posed by the natural environment. The exploration of this location has given us a deep new respect for the bravery and foresight of the individuals responsible for laying the groundwork for the Roanoke colony.

## The "Virginea Pars" Map

The "Virginea Pars" map is a key piece of the jigsaw directly tied to John White. This map was uncovered in addition to the physical items and constructions unearthed at the Roanoke site. This map, which White crafted, is a precise picture of the eastern coast of North America. It includes Roanoke Island and the region around it.

The "Virginea Pars" map represents more than just the land's geography; it is also a historical and cultural treasure. It offers a visual record of the New World as seen through the eyes of John White, a man who was a colonist and a well-known mapper. John White was one of the first to draw maps of the Americas.

As a historian of the New World, White made significant

contributions, and this map is a testimony to those accomplishments. It depicts indigenous communities, flora, animals, and geological elements. It is important because it provides a visual record of the interactions that the colonists had with the native inhabitants of the area. We get a glimpse of the Roanoke colony's surroundings and residents as they looked in the late 16th century, thanks to the deft hand of White, who wrote these accounts.

In addition, the "Virginea Pars" map is a piece of historical data that has the potential to give crucial insights into the outcome of the Roanoke colony. These insights might be used to determine the colony's destiny. It may conceal cryptic hints or identifying markers that might provide insight into the colonists' goals or their final destination. The map is an intriguing relic that begs for more investigation and scrutiny as part of the never-ending search for Roanoke's hidden mysteries.

The archaeological investigations that have been taking place at the Roanoke site have been like a trip of discovery, as they have unearthed the tangible traces of a previously unknown chapter in history. Broken pieces of pottery and tools, as well as the location of the first fort, have provided insight into the routine lives and astonishing resiliency of the Roanoke colonists. They illustrate the human capacity for innovation and industry, as well as the tenacity of the human spirit.

The "Virginea Pars" map that John White made is a witness to the cultural interactions that the colonists had and White's work as a mapper in general. It is a priceless relic that connects us to the past and provides a visual story of the New World as the early residents of Roanoke understood it.

These findings not only add to what we already know about the Roanoke colony, but they also make the enigma more intriguing. As we find relics from the past, we are reminded that history is a never-ending journey, an investigation into the past that continually reveals new details about its mysteries. The Roanoke colony, with all of its unsolved questions and enticing evidence, continues to attract academics and fans to explore further into its mysterious past, holding the promise that one day, the definitive outcome of what happened to the lost colony will be disclosed.

# CHAPTER 6

## Native American Perspectives and Modern Investigations

The Roanoke colony, shrouded in secrecy for a long time, invites us to investigate its puzzling history from various angles. While a lot of focus has been placed on the English settlers who mysteriously disappeared without a trace, the viewpoints of Native Americans and the findings of recent investigations provide fresh insights into the mystery that dates back hundreds of years.

## The Croatoan Tribe and Their Possible Role

The secret meaning of the word "CROATOAN," carved into a tree, is at the center of the Roanoke mystery. This one word has sparked interest and discussion over the part that the Croatoan tribe, the original residents of the area surrounding

Roanoke Island, played in the events. Because of the considerable presence of the Croatoan Indian tribe in the region, the question of whether or not they had any role to play in the outcome of the English colonists continues to be a source of mystery and controversy.

The fact that past encounters between the Roanoke colonists and the Croatoan tribe resulted in the formation of cordial relationships adds an extra layer of ambiguity to the enigma. Some hypotheses postulate that the English colonists, confronted with an increasing number of obstacles and a diminishing supply of resources, may have sought shelter or merger with the Croatoan tribe. This hypothesis raises issues concerning the dynamics of their relationships and whether or not the Croatoan people had an important part in determining the colony's outcome.

It is vital to research the history, culture, and interactions of the Croatoan people with the English settlers to understand the role that the Croatoan tribe played in the Roanoke mystery. We get a more nuanced picture of the events on Roanoke Island in the late 16th century due to our comprehension of their way of life, their customs, and their probable links with the colonists.

## Native American Oral Histories

Native American oral histories have arisen as vital sources of knowledge regarding the English settlers' relationships with indigenous tribes, even though historical documents written by the English settlers have been left behind only in scant quantities. These oral traditions, handed down from generation to generation, provide a unique and indigenous viewpoint on the interactions between the Roanoke colonists and the Native American societies.

These oral histories include recollections of contacts with persons who may have been descendants of the Roanoke colonists. These individuals are not specifically identified in the reports. Often handed down over centuries, these tales provide fascinating clues about the colonists' and indigenous peoples' integration and cohabitation. These anecdotes bring to life the human parts of history by providing insights into personal experiences, relationships, and the mutual influences that determined the fate of the Roanoke colony. [These narratives] bring history to life.

Despite their inability to provide definitive answers, oral histories greatly improve our comprehension of the cultural dynamics and exchanges that occurred during that period. They provide a sense of humanity to the historical story by enabling us to sympathize with the experiences of the English settlers and the Native Americans and by shining light on the histories they shared and the obstacles they faced together.

# Modern Technology: LiDAR and DNA Analysis

Contemporary technology has greatly contributed to the investigation conducted to find buried evidence and solve the Roanoke mystery. Scanners that use light detection and ranging technology (LiDAR) and labs that analyze DNA have been particularly useful in this attempt due to the crucial roles that they have played.

## LiDAR Scanning

LiDAR scanning is a remote sensing technology that uses laser pulses to create three-dimensional terrain maps. These maps are very detailed and accurate. LiDAR scanning has proved to be a game-changer about Roanoke Island and its surrounding areas. Researchers are given the ability to see through layers of dirt and plants to uncover previously unknown archaeological features.

These scans have uncovered previously unknown features, including buildings, walkways, and even possible burial grounds. The use of LiDAR technology has broadened the field of archaeological investigation. As a result, archaeologists can now zero in on specific regions of interest and concentrate their excavation efforts on locations with the most potential to provide essential information about the vanished colony.

Since LiDAR scanning is a technique for mapping the non-intrusive and exact terrain, it has proven to be an extremely useful tool in unearthing the mysteries that lie dormant under the surface of Roanoke Island.

## <u>DNA Analysis</u>

The study into the mystery of Roanoke has also made significant progress thanks to the use of a cutting-edge scientific technique known as DNA analysis. Genetic analysis has been performed on people with links to the Roanoke colonists and descendants of local indigenous groups.

The major goal of DNA analysis is to find genetic markers and links that may offer evidence of intermarriage or assimilation between the colonists and Native Americans. This evidence may be obtained via intermarriage or assimilation. By analyzing DNA samples taken from various people and communities, researchers hope to unearth previously unknown genetic connections that may shed light on the history of the colonists and the prospective descendants of those colonists.

Researchers can now trace familial ties and maybe find answers to long-standing concerns concerning the fate of the Roanoke colony thanks to DNA analysis, which provides a unique window into the past.

## Recent Expeditions and Contemporary Findings

The Roanoke enigma has not been relegated to the annals of history; rather, it continues to capture the imaginations of academics, historians, and fans. Recent excursions to Roanoke Island and the regions around it have resulted in the discovery of contemporary artifacts, which have given the search for information about the fate of the lost colony a fresh lease of life.

## The Lost Colony of Roanoke

The current research landscape encompasses a diverse array of different kinds of endeavors. The ongoing archaeological digs have uncovered new artifacts and buildings, which have provided greater insights into the everyday life of the colonists. These insights deepen our comprehension of the difficulties they encountered and the strategies they used to accommodate themselves to their new surroundings.

In addition, cutting-edge technologies like DNA testing and LiDAR mapping continue to shed light on previously unknown aspects of the Roanoke enigma. These technological advancements can uncover hitherto concealed hints and offer a more complete picture of the events on Roanoke Island.

However, many others share a passion for unraveling the enigma of Roanoke, not simply academics and scholars. The history of the vanished colony is now being preserved thanks to the active participation of enthusiasts, historians, and local communities, as well as the financial backing of research programs. Their unwavering commitment guarantees that the memory of the Roanoke colonists will live on for generations to come and that the mystery will continue to be a source of eternal intrigue and investigation.

The mystery of Roanoke is a tale with several facets, and current investigations, in addition to the opinions of Native Americans, contribute greatly to the mystery's complexity. The possibility that the Croatoan tribe had a part, oral histories passed down from Native Americans, and the use of cutting-edge technology like LiDAR and DNA analysis all contribute to the continuing investigation into the colony's disappearance. Recent expeditions and discoveries highlight the unbroken dedication to solving this centuries-old mystery and preserving the heritage of the Roanoke colony for future generations. This devotion was made clear by the fact that the enigma had not been solved.

# Conclusion

## Unraveling the Enigma and the Legacy of Roanoke

Curious minds and enthusiasts from all over the globe continue to be drawn to the Lost Colony of Roanoke because it is a historical mystery tied up in the annals of time. As we come to the close of our trip through the pages of this book, "The Lost Colony of Roanoke: Unraveling the Mystery of the Vanished Settlement," it is necessary to reflect on the multidimensional character of this lasting enigma and its significant influence on our knowledge of history and culture. We have been reading "The Lost Colony of Roanoke: Unraveling the Mystery of the Vanished Settlement."

## The Complexity and Uncertainty of the Roanoke Colony Mystery

Throughout the previous chapters, we have peeled back layers of historical ambiguity and speculation better to understand the Roanoke Colony enigma and its inner workings. A narrative replete with intricacy and ambiguity emerges a story that stubbornly refuses to hand up its secrets without a fight.

The enigma surrounding the Roanoke Colony is unlike any other historical conundrum. It is a puzzle that has stumped generations of academics and historians. As a result, we now have many ideas, each presenting its unique collection of reasons and evidence. The mystery of Roanoke is an example of a historical problem that does not seem to have a clear answer, whether one considers hypotheses of assimilation, relocation, or confrontations with Native Americans.

The lack of historical documents from that period further deepens its mystery. Because of its very nature, historical research sometimes requires meticulously sorting through shards of the past to piece together a consistent narrative using sources that are insufficient, infrequent, and occasionally even in conflict with one another. This difficulty is shown in its most basic form by the Roanoke mystery, which serves as a jarring reminder of the intrinsic restrictions present in our historical knowledge.

Despite this, the Roanoke Colony enigma remains one of the most alluring and persistent historical problems because of its inherent obscurity and intricacy. It serves as a reminder that not all historical problems are intended to be answered unequivocally, and it is a monument to the mysterious quality of history in and of itself. Instead, they provide us with intellectual challenges, ignite our imaginations, and encourage us to explore the unknown.

# The Enduring Fascination and Cultural Impact of Roanoke

The appeal of The Lost Colony of Roanoke is so strong that it defies categorization by either space or time. Over many centuries, it has been the subject of people's fantasies. As a result, it has become a symbol of the mystery and suspense surrounding historical events that resound with academics and the general public. But what is it about this abandoned community that continues to capture the imagination of people all over the world?

The fact that the Roanoke Colony mystery represents an actual historical riddle adds to its fascination. This mystery has real-world repercussions and real people's lives at its center, so it's hard not to be intrigued. It is a problem that invites us to unravel its complexity, comprehend its cryptic signs, and look for solutions to problems that have endured for ages. The mystery of Roanoke compels us to use our intelligence, forcing us to engage in critical thinking, draw our conclusions, and make connections between seemingly unrelated events.

In addition, the legacy of Roanoke goes beyond the importance that it had in the past. It symbolizes the era of exploration, a time in history characterized by daring journeys into the unknown. In every sense, the colonists who risked their lives to go to Roanoke Island and establish a new settlement there may be considered pioneers. They exemplified the adventurous spirit, the desire to journey into unexplored terrain, and the drive to make a new life for themselves in a faraway country.

In addition, the mystery of Roanoke sheds light on the significance of cross-cultural communication and the intricate workings of the relationships between many communities. The interactions between English settlers and the native peoples of the area illustrate a historical period in which different cultures came into contact with one another, blended, and impacted one another. The history of Roanoke may be seen as a miniature version of the larger tale of cultural exchange that has played a significant role in the development of the globe.

## The Call for Continued Research and Exploration

One clear message emerges as we stand on the brink of ending our investigation into the enigma surrounding the Roanoke Colony: the search for answers is not even finished. The fact that this historical problem is shrouded in mystery and obscurity only invites curious minds, dogged researchers, and future generations to take up the torch and keep moving forward on the road to knowledge.

The enigma of Roanoke is a puzzle that will never become obsolete for either academics or fans. It is a problem that refuses to submit to the passage of time, a puzzle that calls us to investigate more, explore further, and search for the elusive truth. Even if the enigma may never be completely unraveled, looking for solutions deepens our comprehension of human history and the human condition.

The ongoing investigation and investigation into the Roanoke mystery is something that we support, promote, and push for. The scope of what is possible has significantly broadened in recent years thanks to technological developments and the proliferation of cross-disciplinary work. New lines of inquiry are opening up thanks to technologies such as LiDAR scanning and DNA analysis, enabling us to look into the past with unparalleled detail.

The mysteries of Roanoke can only be solved by the cooperation of experts from various fields. It is necessary for specialists from a wide variety of subjects, including history, archaeology, genetics, linguistics, anthropology, and others, to gather together and discuss their unique perspectives and knowledge. We have the greatest chance of putting the pieces of the Roanoke jigsaw together if we draw on the insights and experiences of people from various backgrounds and walks of life.

The voyage is a monument to the ever-present human spirit of exploration and discovery, even if the mystery of the Roanoke Colony may never be solved. It serves as a timely reminder that history is not a fixed record but rather a dynamic tale that is always changing and continues to expose its mysteries with each new finding.

## The Lost Colony of Roanoke

Ultimately, the Lost Colony of Roanoke is a metaphor for our insatiable need for information and our unrelenting dedication to investigating the truth. It is a puzzle that tests us, motivates us, and encourages us to go on an adventure that will never end: a journey to solve the riddle and protect the heritage of people who disappeared into the annals of history on Roanoke Island. We, the curious and the dogged, have been entrusted with the responsibility of carrying on the heritage of Roanoke and ensuring that the voyage of discovery will be continued for future generations.

# CCM Waterston-Hillier